Now *specially recorded arrangements*

tenor saxophone

TAKE THE LEAD

tenor saxophone

International MUSIC Publications

International Music Publications Limited
Griffin House 161 Hammersmith Road London W6 8BS England

DON'T BE A MUSIC COPYCAT!

The copying of © copyright material is a criminal offence and may lead to prosecution.

Series Editor: Sadie Cook

Editorial, production and recording: Artemis Music Limited
Design and production: Space DPS Limited

Published 1999

International MUSIC Publications

© International Music Publications Limited
Griffin House 161 Hammersmith Road London W6 8BS England

Reproducing this music in any form is illegal and forbidden by the Copyright, Designs and Patents Act 1988

IMP

International Music Publications Limited

England:	Griffin House 161 Hammersmith Road London W6 8BS
Germany:	Marstallstr. 8 D-80539 München
Denmark:	Danmusik Vognmagergade 7 DK1120 Copenhagen K

Carisch

Italy:	Via Campania 12 20098 San Giuliano Milanese Milano
Spain:	Magallanes 25 28015 Madrid
France:	20 Rue de la Ville-l'Eveque 75008 Paris

tenor saxophone

TAKE THE LEAD

In the Book...

She Caught The Katy And Left Me A Mule To Ride 6

Gimme Some Lovin' 8

Shake A Tail Feather 12

Everybody Needs Somebody To Love .. 10

The Old Landmark 15

Think 18

Minnie The Moocher 20

Sweet Home Chicago 22

On the CD...

Track **1**   Tuning Tones (A Concert)

She Caught The Katy
And Left Me A Mule To Ride

Track **2**   Full version

Track **3**   Backing track

Gimme Some Lovin'

Track **4**   Full version

Track **5**   Backing track

Shake A Tail Feather

Track **6**   Full version

Track **7**   Backing track

Everybody Needs Somebody To Love

Track **8**   Full version

Track **9**   Backing track

The Old Landmark

Track **10**   Full version

Track **11**   Backing track

Think

Track **12**   Full version

Track **13**   Backing track

Minnie The Moocher

Track **14**   Full version

Track **15**   Backing track

Sweet Home Chicago

Track **16**   Full version

Track **17**   Backing track

She Caught The Katy And Left Me A Mule To Ride

Words and Music by
Taj Mahal and Yank Rachel

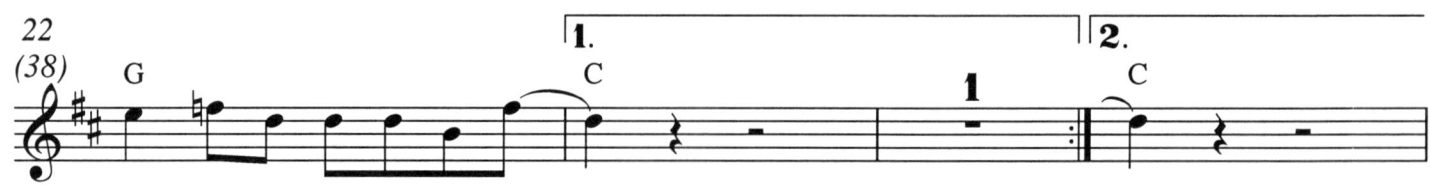

© 1968 & 1999 EMI Blackwood Music Inc and Big Toots Tunes, USA
EMI Songs Ltd, London WC2H 0EA

Gimme Some Lovin'

Demonstration

Backing

Words and Music by Steve Winwood,
Muff Winwood and Spencer Davis

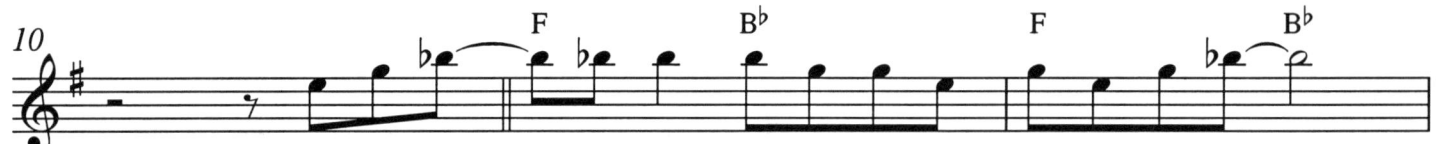

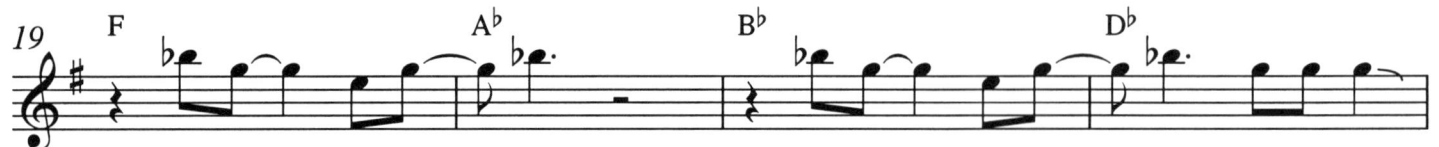

© 1966 & 1999 F.S. Music Ltd/Warner/Chappell Music Ltd, London W6 8BS
and Island Music Ltd, London W6 8JA

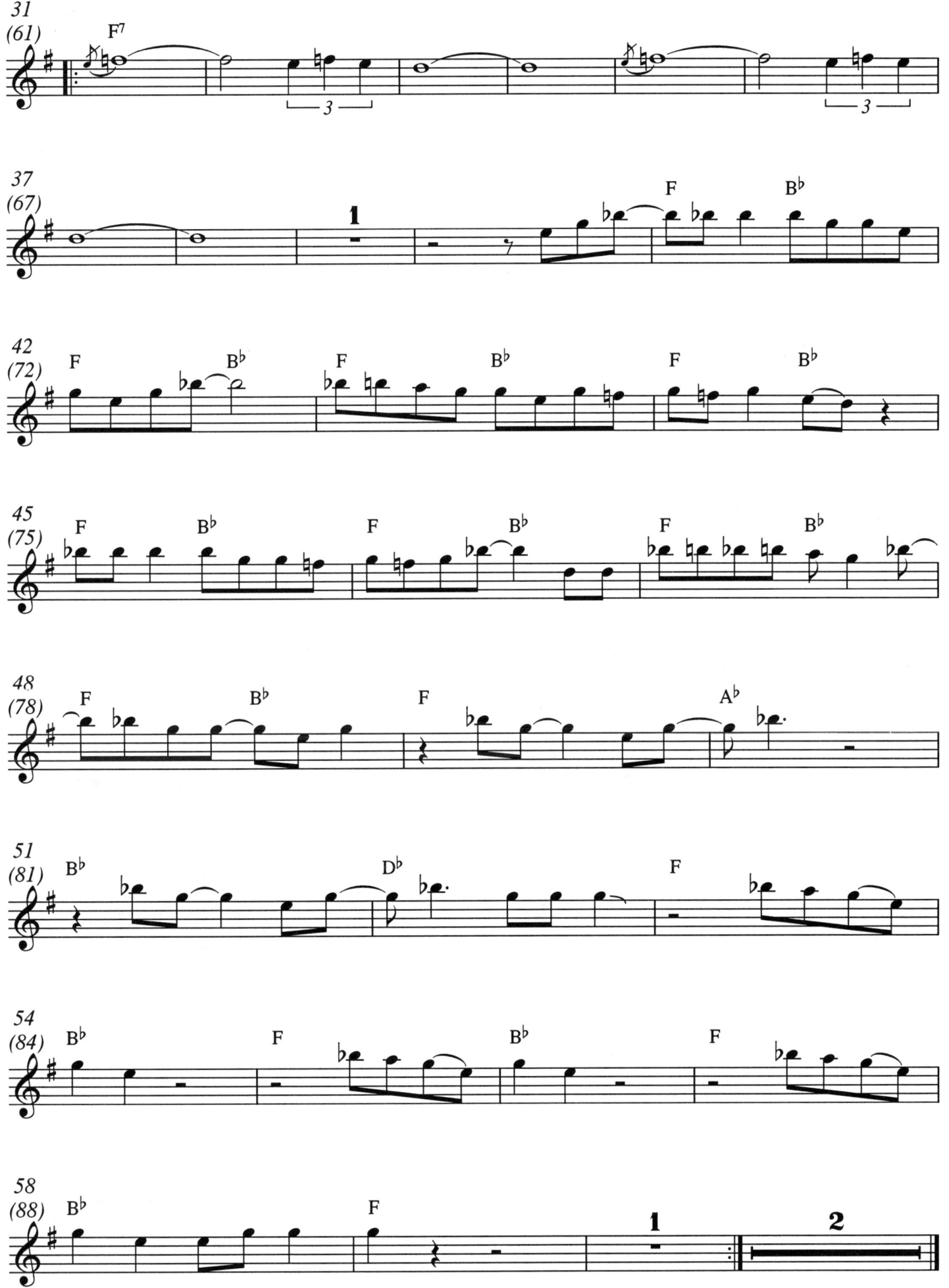

Demonstration

Backing

Everybody Needs Somebody To Love

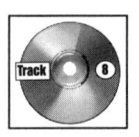

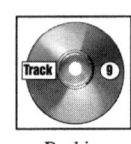

Words and Music by Bert Berns,
Solomon Burke and Jerry Wexler

Bright tempo (♫ = ♩ ♪ triplet)

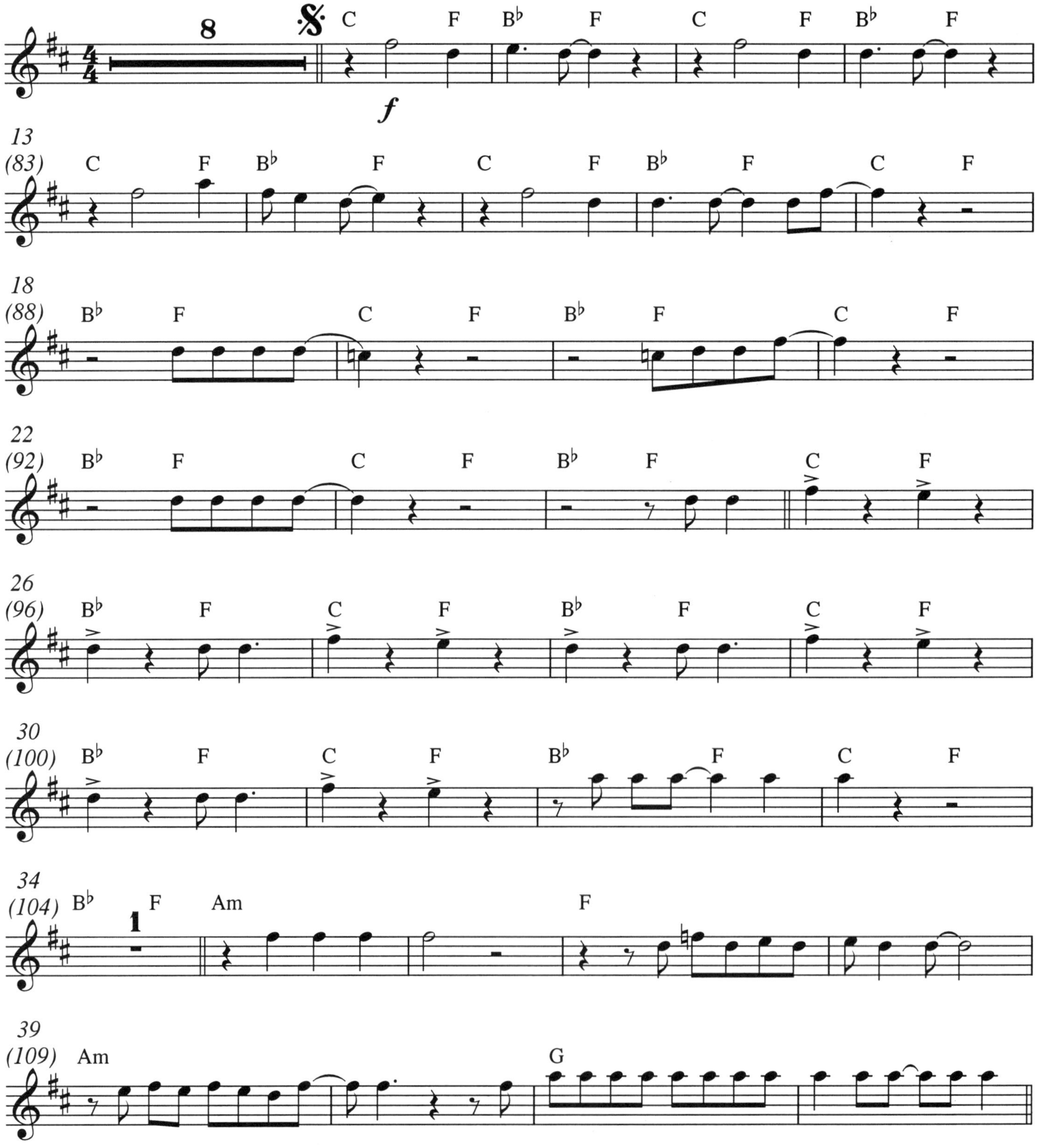

Shake A Tail Feather

Demonstration

Backing

Words and Music by Otis Hayes,
Andre Williams and Verlie Rice

© 1966 Vapac Music Publishing Co, USA
© 1967 Edward Kassner Music Co Ltd, London EC1R 0JH
This arrangement © 1999

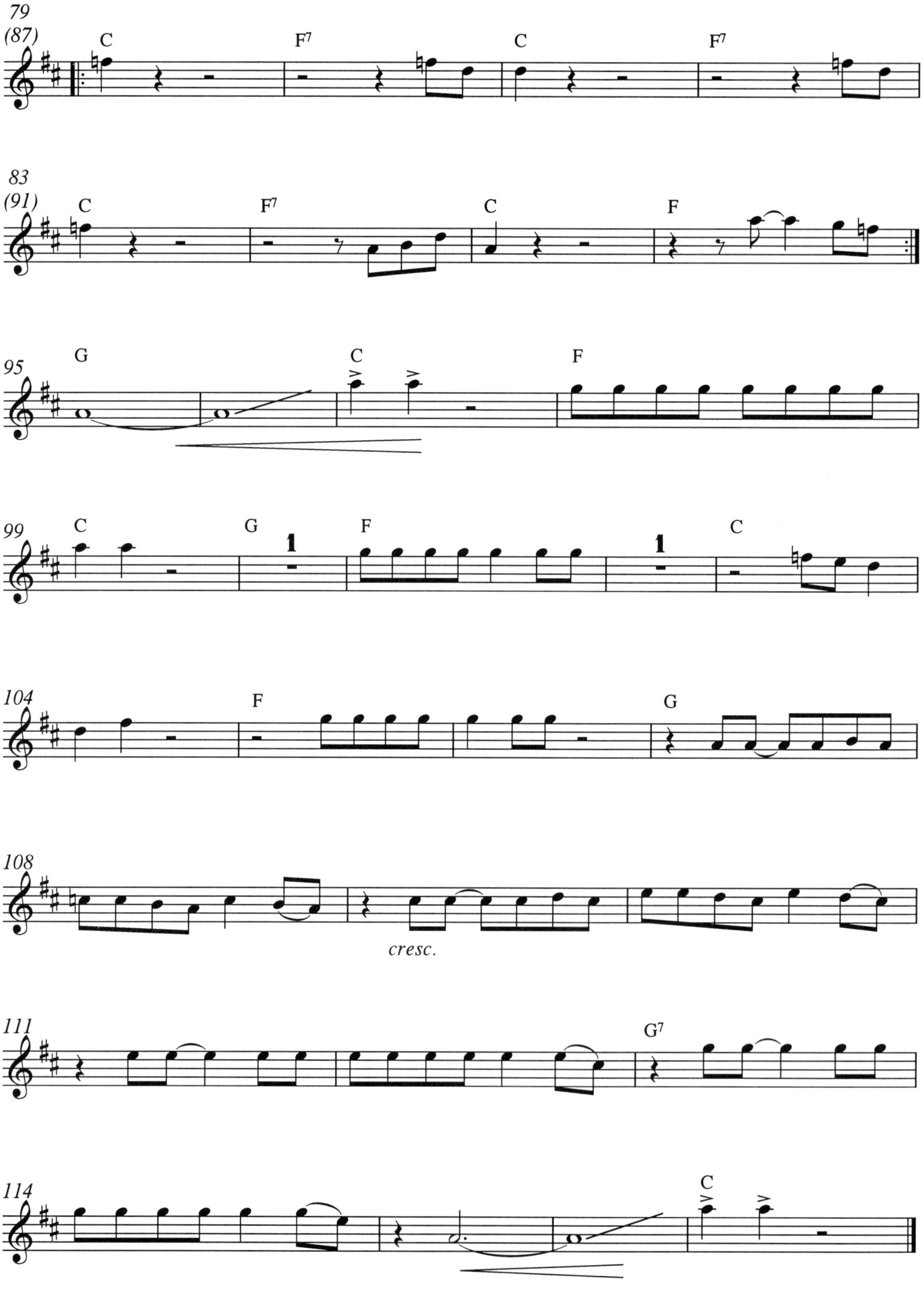
79
(87)
C
F7
C
F7
83
(91)
C
F7
C
F
95
G
C
F
99
C
G
1
F
1
C
104
F
G
108
cresc.
111
G7
114
C

The Old Landmark

Demonstration

Backing

Words and Music by Adeline M Brunner

© 1952 & 1999 Screen Gems-EMI Music Inc, USA
Screen Gems-EMI Music Ltd, London WC2H 0EA

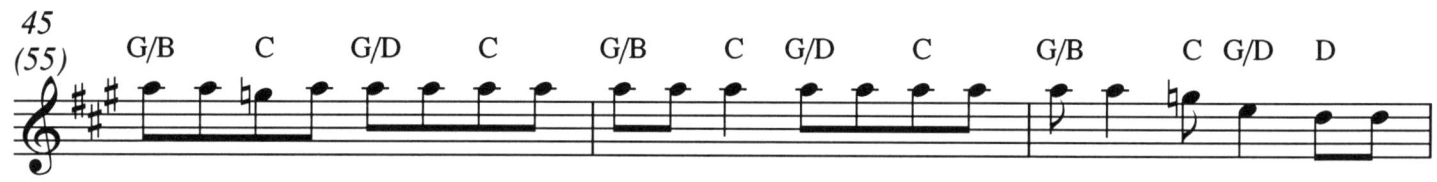

Think

Demonstration

Backing

Words and Music by
Ted White and Aretha Franklin

© 1968 & 1999 Fourteenth Hour Music Corp and Pundit Music, USA
EMI Songs Ltd, London WC2H 0EA

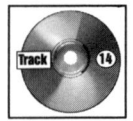

Demonstration

Backing

Minnie The Moocher

Words and Music by Cab Calloway,
Irving Mills and Clarence Gaskill

Medium swing

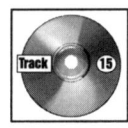

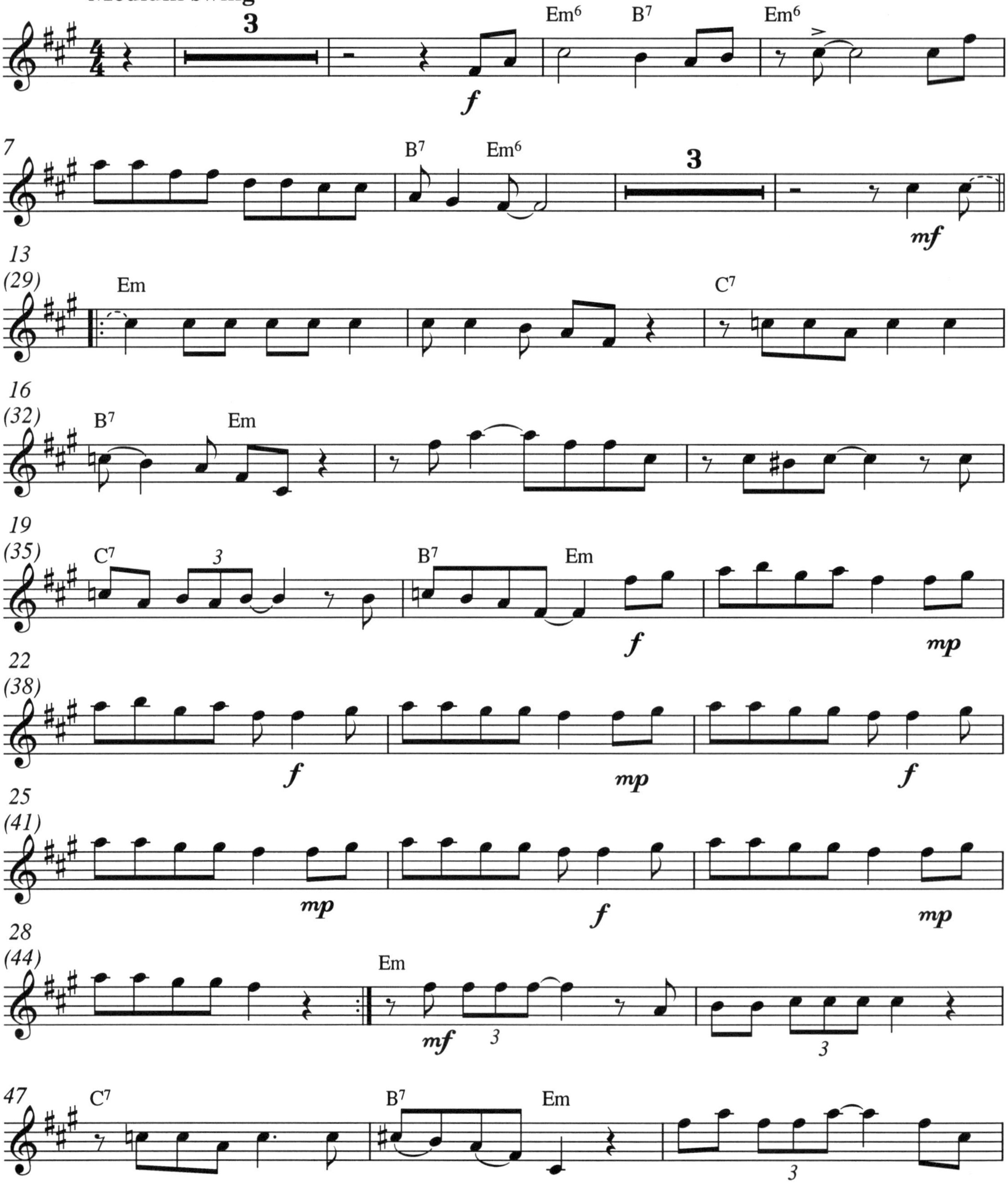

Demonstration

Backing

Sweet Home Chicago

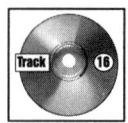

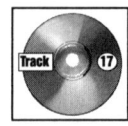

Words and Music by Robert Johnson

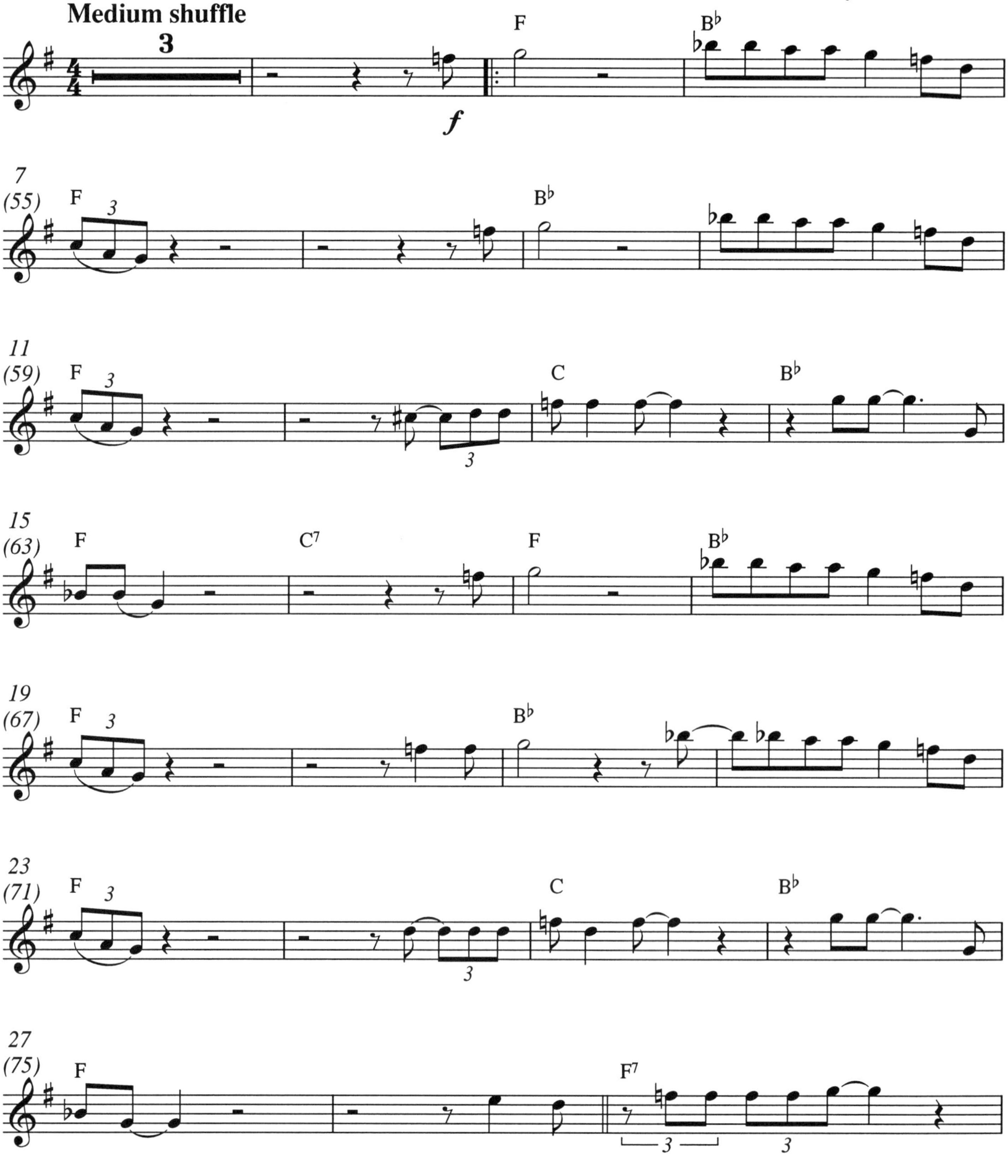

You can be the featured soloist with TAKE THE LEAD

Collect these titles, each with demonstration and full backing tracks on CD.

90s Hits

The Air That I Breathe
(Simply Red)

Angels
(Robbie Williams)

How Do I Live
(LeAnn Rimes)

I Don't Want To Miss A Thing
(Aerosmith)

I'll Be There For You
(The Rembrandts)

My Heart Will Go On
(Celine Dion)

Something About The Way You Look Tonight
(Elton John)

Frozen
(Madonna)

Order ref: 6725A – Flute
Order ref: 6726A – Clarinet
Order ref: 6727A – Alto Saxophone
Order ref: 6728A – Violin

Movie Hits

Because You Loved Me
(Up Close And Personal)

Blue Monday
(The Wedding Singer)

(Everything I Do) I Do It For You
(Robin Hood: Prince Of Thieves)

I Don't Want To Miss A Thing
(Armageddon)

I Will Always Love You
(The Bodyguard)

Star Wars (Main Title)
(Star Wars)

The Wind Beneath My Wings
(Beaches)

You Can Leave Your Hat On
(The Full Monty)

Order ref: 6908A – Flute
Order ref: 6909A – Clarinet
Order ref: 6910A – Alto Saxophone
Order ref: 6911A – Tenor Saxophone
Order ref: 6912A – Violin

TV Themes

Coronation Street

I'll Be There For You
(theme from *Friends*)

Match Of The Day

(Meet) The Flintstones

Men Behaving Badly

Peak Practice

The Simpsons

The X-Files

Order ref: 7003A – Flute
Order ref: 7004A – Clarinet
Order ref: 7005A – Alto Saxophone
Order ref: 7006A – Violin

Christmas Songs

The Christmas Song (Chestnuts Roasting On An Open Fire)

Frosty The Snowman

Have Yourself A Merry Little Christmas

Little Donkey

Rudolph The Red-Nosed Reindeer

Santa Claus Is Comin' To Town

Sleigh Ride

Winter Wonderland

Order ref: 7022A – Flute
Order ref: 7023A – Clarinet
Order ref: 7024A – Alto Saxophone
Order ref: 7025A – Violin
Order ref: 7026A – Piano
Order ref: 7027A – Drums

The Blues Brothers

She Caught The Katy And Left Me A Mule To Ride

Gimme Some Lovin'

Shake A Tail Feather

Everybody Needs Somebody To Love

The Old Landmark

Think

Minnie The Moocher

Sweet Home Chicago

Order ref: 7079A - Flute
Order ref: 7080A - Clarinet
Order ref: 7081A - Alto Saxophone
Order ref: 7082A - Tenor Saxophone
Order ref: 7083A - Trumpet
Order ref: 7084A - Violin